the *Lord*

Has Made

© 2013 by Barbour Publishing, Inc.

Written and compiled by Joanna Bloss.

Print ISBN 978-1-62416-139-1

eBook Editions:
Adobe Digital Edition (.epub) 978-1-62416-495-8
Kindle and MobiPocket Edition (.prc) 978-1-62416-494-1

Published by Barbour Publishing, Inc., P.O. Box 719, Uhrichsville, Ohio 44683, www.barbourbooks.com

Our mission is to publish and distribute inspirational products offering exceptional value and biblical encouragement to the masses.

Member of the
Evangelical Christian
Publishers Association

Printed in the United States of America.

This is the Day
the *Lord*
Has Made

Inspiration for Women

BARBOUR
PUBLISHING

Contents

Introduction

This is the day the Lord has made.
We will rejoice and be glad in it.

PSALM 118:24 NLT

Live in the moment. From television commercials to eulogies, we are reminded to squeeze every drop of joy from the current moment. So why is it such a temptation for us to become snagged in the past or get obsessed with the future? When we are busy looking back or preoccupied with straining forward, the present can quickly be swallowed up and lost. While God wants us to live on earth with a constant eye on eternity, He is also quite concerned with the *now*. Living in the moment, we learn to relate to Him and others, to be obedient, and to live out our faith through whatever life brings. As you reflect on these readings, ask God to flood your soul with joy. . .immersed in *this* day, *this* hour, *this* precious moment in time.

JOY
in
Forgiveness

*Jesus stepped into a boat, crossed over
and came to his own town. Some men brought
to him a paralyzed man, lying on a mat.
When Jesus saw their faith, he said to the man,
"Take heart, son; your sins are forgiven."*

MATTHEW 9:1–3 NIV

It isn't clear why the man couldn't walk. Perhaps he
was born that way; perhaps his condition was the
result of a terrible accident. Scripture only tells us he
was paralyzed, unable to get to where he wanted to
go without the aid of friends. Jesus was moved by
their faith, and true to His character, He addresses
the heart before the body: "Your sins are forgiven."
As a result, the man experienced both a spiritual and
a physical healing that day. What unspeakable joy.

How often do our hearts become paralyzed over past sins? A kind word unspoken, a failure to act, a grievous error causing shame and regret. We can become so consumed with our failures that we can no longer move forward. We become depressed, empty of joy. When it comes to our past, God makes His intent clear: There is no condemnation for the children of God. Our sins are cast as far as the east is from the west. This is good news, bringing with it freedom from the chains of darkness. When we come to God in faith, He heals our hearts and frees us to walk, to run, to move forward joyfully for Him.

Let God's forgiveness break the chains of your past, bringing joy to your present.

He is so rich in kindness and grace that
he purchased our freedom with the blood
of his Son and forgave our sins.

EPHESIANS 1:7 NLT

"If my people, who are called by my name,
will humble themselves and pray and seek my
face and turn from their wicked ways, then
will I hear from heaven, and I will forgive
their sin and will heal their land."

2 CHRONICLES 7:14 NIV

As far as the east is from the west, so far
has he removed our transgressions from us.

PSALM 103:12 NIV

To be a Christian means to forgive
the inexcusable because God has
forgiven the inexcusable in you.
C.S. LEWIS

To err is human; to forgive, divine.
ALEXANDER POPE

After grief for sin there should
be joy for forgiveness.
A. W. PINK

Forgiveness does not change the past,
but it does enlarge the future.
PAUL BOESE

Joy in Forgiveness

Be kind to each other, tenderhearted,
forgiving one another, just as God
through Christ has forgiven you.

EPHESIANS 4:32 NLT

Forgiveness is an interesting thing. When you
release someone from the sin he or she has
committed against you, it's almost like setting
a bird free from a cage. You've freed that
person up to soar. And, in doing so, you've
also freed yourself up. No longer do you have
to hold on to the bitterness or anger. Letting
go means you can truly move forward with
your life. . .in joy!

Sweet Freedom

Father, when I feel guilty and ashamed for my past behavior, I am tempted to think You must want me to suffer miserably for my sin. But Your word tells me forgiveness is mine for the asking. I have asked—now help me be done with remorse and shame. Thank You for the freedom that forgiveness brings. Thank You for the joy of a new, clean heart. Amen.

*O Lord, you are so good, so ready
to forgive, so full of unfailing love
for all who ask for your help.*

PSALM 86:5 NLT

*So now, there is no condemnation
for those who belong to Christ Jesus.
And because you belong to him, the power
of the life-giving Spirit has freed you from the
power of sin that leads to death.*

ROMANS 8:1–2 NLT

*You have turned my mourning into joyful
dancing. You have taken away my clothes
of mourning and clothed me with joy.*

PSALM 30:11 NLT

*"Forgive Your people Israel whom
You have redeemed, O Lᴏʀᴅ, and do not
place the guilt of innocent blood in the
midst of your people Israel." And the
bloodguiltiness shall be forgiven them.*

Dᴇᴜᴛᴇʀᴏɴᴏᴍʏ 21:8 ɴᴀsʙ

*Take words with you and return to the
Lᴏʀᴅ. Say to him: "Forgive all our sins
and receive us graciously, that we
may offer the fruit of our lips."*

Hᴏsᴇᴀ 14:2 ɴɪᴠ

*Feel my pain and see my trouble.
Forgive all my sins.*

Psᴀʟᴍ 25:18 ɴʟᴛ

Joyous Freedom

*How blessed is he whose transgression
is forgiven, whose sin is covered!*

PSALM 32:1 NASB

What if you were locked up in a prison cell
for years on end? You waited for the day
when the jailer would turn that key in the
lock—releasing you once and for all. In a
sense, experiencing God's forgiveness is like
being set free from prison. Can you fathom
the joy? Walking into the sunshine for the
first time in years? Oh praise Him for His
forgiveness today!

The Gift of Grace

*Heavenly Father, it brings such joy
to know that Your grace is greater than
all my sin. I am overwhelmed by this gift,
new each morning. Your grace carries me
through the day and tucks me into Your
everlasting arms when my head hits the
pillow each night. Thank You for
Your amazing grace. Amen.*

I think that if God forgives us we
must forgive ourselves. Otherwise,
it is almost like setting ourselves up
as a higher tribunal than Him.

C.S. Lewis

Forgiveness is an act of the will,
and the will can function regardless
of the temperature of the heart.

Corrie ten Boom

God pardons like a mother,
who kisses the offense into
everlasting forgiveness.

Henry Ward Beecher

JOY
in the
Moment

*"Therefore do not worry about tomorrow,
for tomorrow will worry about itself.
Each day has enough trouble of its own."*
MATTHEW 6:34 NIV

Unfortunately, worry seems to be a part of the
human condition. We've become so accustomed
to worry that when we're not worrying, we start to
wonder if we are missing something important! We
worry about the past, the things we should have
done but didn't, and the things others have done to
us. We worry about the future, what might happen
when, and how it may impact us. When we focus on
the past we become depressed—weighed down by
burdens, by circumstances that can't be changed.
This weight keeps us from moving forward. When
we focus on the future, we become anxious—
worried about what tomorrow may bring, wondering
how we might prevent any catastrophe.

In stark contrast to the way many of us are naturally wired, Jesus challenges His children to focus on the present. This moment. This day. Our past is forgiven, woven into the tapestry of our Creator's loving hands. Our future is secure, held tight in His everlasting arms.

It takes practice to face each day with an absence of worry about yesterday and a refusal to obsess about tomorrow. But concentrating on the present brings the rich reward of freedom from anxiety and depression. It provides joy—a calm assurance—and allows us to walk hand-in-hand with the One who is with us each step of the way.

When anxiety was great within me,
your consolation brought me joy.

PSALM 94:19 NIV

Why, my soul, are you downcast? Why so
disturbed within me? Put your hope in God,
for I will yet praise him, my Savior and my God.

PSALM 42:5 NIV

"So don't worry about these things, saying,
'What will we eat? What will we drink?
What will we wear?' These things dominate
the thoughts of unbelievers, but your heavenly
Father already knows all your needs."

MATTHEW 6:31–32 NLT

The most wasted of all days
is one without laughter.
E. E. CUMMINGS

Hope frees us from the need to predict
the future and allows us to live in the
present, with the deep trust that God will
never leave us alone but will fulfill the
deepest desires of our heart. . . . Joy in this
perspective is the fruit of hope.
HENRI J. M. NOUWEN

Let a joy keep you. Reach out your
hands and take it when it runs by.
CARL SANDBURG

Comparison is the thief of joy.
MARK TWAIN

Know My Heart

Search me, O God, and know my heart;
test me and know my anxious thoughts.

PSALM 139:23 NLT

Have you ever asked the Lord to give you an
"anxiety check"? He longs for you to live in
peace, but that won't happen as long as you're
driven by worries and fears. Today, allow Him
to search your heart. Ask Him to dig deep.
Are there cobwebs that need to be swept out?
Things hidden that should be revealed? Let
God wash away your anxieties, replacing them
with His exceeding great joy!

Calm My Anxious Heart

Father, I confess that I am prone to worry. My mind seems to naturally ruminate over past sins and obsess over future fears. I recognize that this worry causes depression and anxiety, and these things overtake my soul and keep me from looking to You. Forgive me for straying down this dark path. Cleanse and calm my anxious heart, draw my gaze gently to Your loving eyes. Amen.

When my anxious thoughts multiply within me, Your consolations delight my soul.

Psalm 94:19 NASB

Don't worry about anything; instead, pray about everything. Tell God what you need, and thank him for all he has done.

Philippians 4:6 NLT

"But you are obsessed with whether the godless will be judged. Don't worry, judgment and justice will be upheld."

Job 36:17 NLT

*Humble yourselves, therefore, under
God's mighty hand, that he may lift you
up in due time. Cast all your anxiety
on him because he cares for you.*

1 PETER 5:6–7 NIV

*Let my soul be at rest again,
for the LORD has been good to me.*

PSALM 116:7 NLT

*But I have calmed and quieted myself,
I am like a weaned child with its mother;
like a weaned child I am content.*

PSALM 131:2 NIV

Sing, O Heavens!

*Shout for joy, you heavens; rejoice,
you earth; burst into song, you mountains!
For the L*ORD* comforts his people and will
have compassion on his afflicted ones.*

ISAIAH 49:13 NIV

Imagine you're walking through a meadow
on a dewy morning. The sweet smell of dawn
lingers in the air. Suddenly, like a skilled
orchestra, the heavens above begin to pour
out an unexpected song of joy. You close
your eyes, overwhelmed by the majesty of
the moment. Scripture tells us the heavens
and the earth are joyful. . .so tune in to their
chorus today.

Through a Child's Eyes

*Father, just for today, help me to see Your
world through a child's eyes. Help me to live
in the moment of brilliant blue skies, the
warm sun on my face, the gentle whisper
of a butterfly's wings. Sharpen my senses
so I don't miss a single thing, free to
run and play and embrace all the beauty
this day and this hour hold for me. Amen.*

Joy is the infallible sign
of the presence of God.

PIERRE TEILHARD DE CHARDIN

A thing of beauty is a joy forever.

JOHN KEATS

There is not one blade of grass,
there is no color in this world that
is not intended to make us rejoice.

JOHN CALVIN

JOY
in
Obedience

But Jonah ran away from the Lord *and headed for Tarshish. He went down to Joppa, where he found a ship bound for that port. After paying the fare, he went aboard and sailed for Tarshish to flee from the* Lord.

JONAH 1:3 NIV

Have you ever known that God wanted you to do something specific, but you just didn't want to do it? Perhaps you felt ill-equipped, untrained, or unprepared for the task ahead. Perhaps you were fearful of the outcome, placing too much of the burden and responsibility on yourself for how things would turn out.

When God asked him to go to Nineveh and preach against the wickedness there, Jonah quickly made other plans. Perhaps he felt foolish or didn't know what to say or how to say it, or maybe he was just plain scared. Regardless, "Jonah ran away from the Lord" (Jonah 1:3 NIV). Such disobedience is not an uncommon response. When we run from the Lord, it may well mean we are limiting ourselves based on our past experiences or our perceptions of what we can do. We are putting too much thought into our own resources rather than focusing on God's incomparable power. True obedience demands that we step outside of ourselves and our thoughts about what seems humanly possible. It insists we adopt a more God-like perspective, focusing on His ability to equip and empower us to do abundantly more than we could ever ask or imagine.

*For we are God's handiwork, created in
Christ Jesus to do good works, which God
prepared in advance for us to do.*

EPHESIANS 2:10 NIV

*But he said to me, "My grace is sufficient
for you, for my power is made perfect
in weakness." Therefore I will boast all
the more gladly about my weaknesses,
so that Christ's power may rest on me.*

2 CORINTHIANS 12:9 NIV

*By God's grace and mighty power,
I have been given the privilege of serving
him by spreading this Good News.*

EPHESIANS 3:7 NLT

The joy of Jesus was His absolute
self-surrender and self-sacrifice to
His Father—the joy of doing that
which the Father sent Him to do.

OSWALD CHAMBERS

Happiness is not a goal. . .
it's a by-product of a life well-lived.

ELEANOR ROOSEVELT

What is peculiar in the life of a man
consists not in his obedience, but his
opposition to his instincts. In one
direction or another he strives to
live a supernatural life.

HENRY DAVID THOREAU

Joyful Obedience

Now to Him who is able to keep you from
stumbling, and to make you stand in the
presence of His glory blameless with great joy. . .
JUDE 24 NASB

Our obedience makes God happy and should
make us happy, too. In fact, the more difficult
it is to obey, the more joyful we should be.
Why? Because a big situation calls for a big
God. And our God is bigger than anything
we could ask or think. He alone can prevent
us from falling. So, if you're struggling in the
area of obedience, surrender your will. Enter
into joyful obedience.

Obedience Makes Me Glad

*Jesus, sometimes it's hard to obey. Even when
I know You're prompting me to act, to forgive,
or to serve, I sometimes want to sail away on a
metaphorical ship as far from You as possible.
During those times, when I long to escape,
I feel miserable! Even so, I know from personal
experience that when I obey You, it makes me
glad! And it makes You glad, too. Infuse my
heart with a desire to obey. Amen.*

Then God said to Abraham, "Your responsibility is to obey the terms of the covenant. You and all your descendants have this continual responsibility."

GENESIS 17:9 NLT

And the people said to Joshua, "We will serve the LORD our God and obey him."

JOSHUA 24:24 NIV

Samuel said, "Has the LORD as much delight in burnt offerings and sacrifices as in obeying the voice of the LORD? Behold, to obey is better than sacrifice, and to heed than the fat of rams."

1 SAMUEL 15:22 NASB

*"And through your descendants all the
nations of the earth will be blessed—
all because you have obeyed me."*

GENESIS 22:18 NLT

*"If you obey all the decrees and commands
I am giving you today, all will be well with
you and your children. I am giving you these
instructions so you will enjoy a long life in
the land the LORD your God is giving
you for all time."*

DEUTERONOMY 4:40 NLT

*His affection abounds all the more toward you,
as he remembers the obedience of you all,
how you received him with fear and trembling.*

2 CORINTHIANS 7:15 NASB

Give 'Em Something to Talk About

Everyone has heard about your obedience,
so I rejoice because of you; but I want
you to be wise about what is good,
and innocent about what is evil.

ROMANS 16:19 NIV

Ever been caught in a situation where people
were talking about you behind your back?
Maybe folks you loved and trusted? How did
that make you feel? Well, how would you feel
if you found out people were talking about
you. . .because of your obedience? Wow!
That's a different thing altogether. Let them
talk! May our joyful obedience to the Lord win
us a spot in many cheerful conversations!

Look to You

Heavenly Father, it is so much easier to obey when I focus on You rather than what others think of me. I confess my tendency to be a people pleaser, dreading the thought of others misunderstanding me or thinking me a fool. People will not always be happy with me. Especially when I obey You, my actions may not make sense. Just the same, help me keep my eyes focused on You. Amen.

I think we all sin by needlessly disobeying
the apostolic injunction to rejoice
as much as by anything else.

C. S. Lewis

How will you find good? It is not a thing
of choice; it is a river that flows from the
foot of the invisible throne, and flows
by the path of obedience.

George Eliot

One act of obedience is better
than one hundred sermons.

Dietrich Bonhoeffer

Trust and obey
For there's no other way
To be happy in Jesus
But to trust and obey.

John Henry Sammis

JOY
in
Loss

When Mary reached the place where Jesus was and saw him, she fell at his feet and said, "Lord, if you had been here, my brother would not have died." When Jesus saw her weeping, and the Jews who had come along with her also weeping, he was deeply moved in spirit and troubled. "Where have you laid him?" he asked. "Come and see, Lord," they replied. Jesus wept.

JOHN 11:32–35 NIV

Perhaps one of the most moving scenes in the New Testament is when Jesus wept upon greeting Mary after the death of His beloved friend and her brother, Lazarus. Despite knowing He would soon deliver Lazarus from death, Jesus still cried, no doubt moved by the grief of sisters Mary and Martha and deeply sad to see His friends suffering so. In a moment of profound empathy, Jesus embraced His humanity and cried real tears.

Whether it is the loss of a loved one, the loss of a dream unfulfilled, or one never to be, as long as we walk this earth, our hearts simply must endure seasons of grief. Even when we carry with us the big picture, the hope of heaven, and the knowledge that this is temporary pain, we will still shed tears of sadness from time to time. Grief in the face of eternity is bittersweet. Ironically and supernaturally, we can still experience joy, even through tears, when we cling to the hope that God is our comforter and will never, ever, leave us alone.

But you, God, see the trouble of the afflicted;
you consider their grief and take it in hand.
The victims commit themselves to you;
you are the helper of the fatherless.

PSALM 10:14 NIV

For no one is cast off by the Lord forever.
Though he brings grief, he will show
compassion, so great is his unfailing love.
For he does not willingly bring affliction
or grief to anyone.

LAMENTATIONS 3:31–33 NIV

Man is more himself, more manlike,
when joy is the fundamental
thing and grief superficial.

G. K. Chesterton

Instead of weeping when a tragedy
occurs in a songbird's life, it sings away
its grief. I believe we could well follow
the pattern of our feathered friends.

William Shakespeare

Count not thyself to have found true
peace, if thou hast felt no grief; nor that
then all is well if thou hast no adversary;
nor that this is perfect, if all things fall
out according to thy desire.

Honore de Balzac

Beauty for Ashes

Provide for those who grieve in Zion. . .bestow
on them a crown of beauty instead of ashes,
the oil of joy instead of mourning, and a
garment of praise instead of a spirit of despair.
ISAIAH 61:3 NIV

Seasons of mourning are difficult to bear, but
praise God, He promises to give us beauty for
ashes! He pours joy over us like a scented oil. . .
to woo us out of periods of grieving. Can you
feel it washing down on your head, even now?
Can you sense the change in attitude? Slip on
that garment of praise, believer! Shake off the
ashes! Let God's joy overwhelm you!

Never Alone

*Father, no matter how deeply my heart aches,
I thank You that I am never alone. What a
joy to know You walk beside me through the
valley of the shadow of death. I cling to Your
hand, knowing somehow You will guide me
through this long, dark journey of sadness.
Thank You for Your presence and for the joy
it brings in the midst of my pain. Amen.*

Be merciful to me, LORD, for I am in distress;
my eyes grow weak with sorrow,
my soul and body with grief.

PSALM 31:9 NIV

"Go therefore and make disciples of all
the nations, baptizing them in the name
of the Father and the Son and the Holy
Spirit, teaching them to observe all that
I commanded you; and lo, I am with you
always, even to the end of the age."

MATTHEW 28:19–20 NASB

*"Now is your time of grief, but I will
see you again and you will rejoice,
and no one will take away your joy."*

JOHN 16:22 NIV

*In all this you greatly rejoice, though now for
a little while you may have had to suffer grief
in all kinds of trials. These have come so
that the proven genuineness of your faith—of
greater worth than gold, which perishes even
though refined by fire —may result in praise,
glory and honor when Jesus Christ is revealed.*

1 PETER 1:6-7 NIV

The Joy of the Lord Is Your Strength

*"This day is holy to our Lord. Do not grieve,
for the joy of the Lord is your strength."*

NEHEMIAH 8:10 NIV

Is it possible to have joy in the middle of
catastrophic circumstances? What if you're
facing the loss of a job? A devastating illness?
The death of a loved one? Can you really look
beyond your grief to find the joy? Our very
strength comes from the joy God places inside
us, and we need that strength even more
when we're facing seemingly impossible odds!
Today, may God's joy strengthen you from the
inside out.

Thank You for Strength

*Lord, I admit I become sad when I imagine
losing someone I dearly love or when facing
a hardship too great to bear. I become fearful,
asking myself how I could possibly endure
such a loss. In these times, remind me that just
like the sacrifice for Abraham, You will provide
exactly what I need at the precise moment
I need it. Thank You for this yet untapped
reservoir of strength. Amen.*

To me, the human experience does
involve a great deal of anguish. It's joyful,
but it's bittersweet. I just think that's life.

AMY GRANT

I hold it true, whatever befall;
I feel it, when I sorrow most;
'tis better to have loved and lost
than never to have loved at all.

ALFRED LORD TENNYSON

Give sorrow words. The grief
that does not speak whispers the
o'er-fraught heart, and bids it break.

WILLIAM SHAKESPEARE

JOY
in
Pain

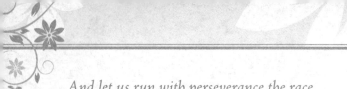

*And let us run with perseverance the race
marked out for us, fixing our eyes on Jesus,
the pioneer and perfecter of faith. For the joy
set before him he endured the cross, scorning
its shame, and sat down at the right
hand of the throne of God.*

HEBREWS 12:1–2 NIV

Crucifixion is easily among the most painful, cruel, and horrific ways for a person to die. It is stunning to consider that Jesus voluntarily surrendered His deity and chose to subject Himself to the greatest depths of human pain. Despite His extreme physical and emotional suffering, Jesus maintained His focus on the "joy set before him," confident that soon He would return to His rightful seat next to the throne of God. Focusing on His Father allowed Jesus to transcend the depths of physical pain and experience peace only God can provide.

A Prayer for Pain

*Father, I hurt. Whether it's physical or
emotional, when one part of me is in pain,
my whole body suffers. When my body suffers,
I think only of my discomfort. I become
whiney, irritable, difficult to live with. Then
the people around me start to suffer. Instead of
dragging it with me, today I surrender my pain
to You. Take it, heal it, and heal me. Amen.*

*I am bent over and racked with pain. All day
long I walk around filled with grief. A raging
fever burns within me, and my health is broken.
I am exhausted and completely crushed.
My groans come from an anguished heart.*

PSALM 38:6–8 NLT

*He was despised and rejected by mankind,
a man of suffering, and familiar with pain.
Like one from whom people hide their faces he
was despised, and we held him in low esteem.*

ISAIAH 53:3 NIV

64

"Then I would still have this consolation—
my joy in unrelenting pain—that I had
not denied the words of the Holy One."

JOB 6:10 NIV

I am suffering and in pain. Rescue me,
O God, by your saving power. Then I will
praise God's name with singing, and I
will honor him with thanksgiving.

PSALM 69:29–30 NLT

No discipline is enjoyable while it is
happening—it's painful! But afterward
there will be a peaceful harvest of right living
for those who are trained in this way.

HEBREWS 12:11 NLT

A New Season

"A woman giving birth to a child has pain because her time has come; but when her baby is born she forgets the anguish because of her joy that a child is born into the world."

JOHN 16:21 NIV

If you've ever delivered a child, you know the pain associated with childbirth. But that's not what you remember after the fact, is it? No, as you hold that little one in your arms, only one thing remains. . .the supernatural joy you experience as you gaze into your newborn's eyes. The same is true with the seasons we walk through. Sorrows will end, and joy will rise to the surface once again!

In a Little While

*Heavenly Father, when I think of eternity,
I know the pain of today will seem a distant
memory of a long-ago past. Right now it
feels eternal, but my mind knows this pain is
temporary. In a little while, this will seem like
a long time ago. Thank You for this constant
reminder that there is more life and joy to
come, oh so much more to come! Amen.*

Joy does not simply happen to us.
We have to choose joy and keep
choosing it every day.

HENRI J.M. NOUWEN

The excursion is the same when you
go looking for your sorrow as when
you go looking for your joy.

EUDORA WELTY

Brave men rejoice in adversity,
just as brave soldiers triumph in war.

LUCIUS ANNAEUS SENECA

Hold on, my child, joy
comes in the morning.

GLORIA GAITHER

JOY
in
Confusion

For God is not a God
of disorder but of peace.
1 Corinthians 14:33 NIV

When Rebekah was pregnant, she noticed some unusual activity in her womb. When she asked God about it, He said something that was likely very confusing: "The sons in your womb will become two nations. From the very beginning, the two nations will be rivals. One nation will be stronger than the other; and your older son [Esau] will serve your younger son [Jacob]" (Genesis 25:23 NLT).

Scripture isn't clear as to whether Rebekah was thinking about this years later when her husband Isaac was in his last days and deemed it time for him to bestow his blessing on their eldest son. Yet Rebekah must have felt considerable anxiety. Her fretfulness seemingly led to her bold intervention, which brought disorder to her family and nearly caused Jacob his life (see Genesis 27).

Confusion can cause anxiety within us, a sense of urgency to act, to do *something*, even when it isn't clear what that something should be. Making decisions from a place of anxiety often causes even more problems, as it certainly did for Isaac, Rebekah, Jacob, and Esau.

God does not always make His plans crystal clear to us, but when we pause to listen to His leading and trust Him for the outcome, we can be confident He will never lead us in a way of disorder, but of calm, perfect peace.

Anxiety weighs down the heart,
but a kind word cheers it up.

PROVERBS 12:25 NIV

We may throw the dice, but the
LORD determines how they fall.

PROVERBS 16:33 NLT

My mouth will speak words of wisdom;
the meditation of my heart will
give you understanding.

PSALM 49:3 NIV

The fear of the LORD is the beginning of
wisdom; all who follow his precepts have good
understanding. To him belongs eternal praise.

PSALM 111:10 NIV

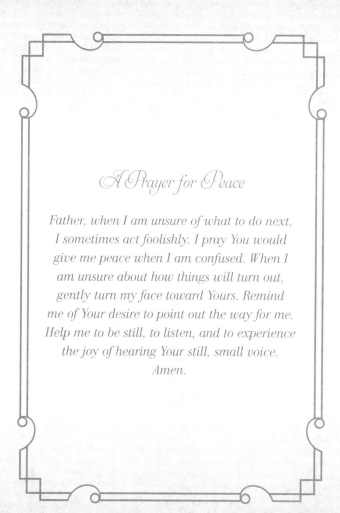

A Prayer for Peace

Father, when I am unsure of what to do next,
I sometimes act foolishly. I pray You would
give me peace when I am confused. When I
am unsure about how things will turn out,
gently turn my face toward Yours. Remind
me of Your desire to point out the way for me.
Help me to be still, to listen, and to experience
the joy of hearing Your still, small voice.
Amen.

*My child, listen to what I say, and treasure
my commands. Tune your ears to wisdom,
and concentrate on understanding. Cry
out for insight, and ask for understanding.
Search for them as you would for silver;
seek them like hidden treasures.*

PROVERBS 2:1–4 NLT

*"Choose my instruction instead of silver,
knowledge rather than choice gold,
for wisdom is more precious than rubies,
and nothing you desire can compare with her.
I, wisdom, dwell together with prudence;
I possess knowledge and discretion."*

PROVERBS 8:10–12 NIV

"Joy" in Philippians is a defiant
"Nevertheless!" that Paul sets like a full
stop against the Philippians' anxiety.

KARL BARTH

Joy is distinctly a Christian word and
a Christian thing. It is a reverse of
happiness. Happiness is the result of what
happens of an agreeable sort. Joy has its
spring deep down inside, and that spring
never runs dry, no matter what happens.
Only Jesus gives that joy.

SAMUEL GORDON

The Key to Happiness

*Those who listen to [wise] instruction
will prosper; those who trust in
the LORD will be joyful.*

PROVERBS 16:20 NKJV

Want the key to true happiness? Try wisdom.
When others around you are losing their
heads, losing their cool, and losing sleep over
their decisions, choose to be different. Step
up to the plate. Handle matters wisely. Wise
choices always lead to joyous outcomes. And
along the way, you will be setting an example
for others around you to follow. So, c'mon. . .
get happy! Get wisdom!

Make Me Wise

*Father, the worldly path to wisdom is lined
with chatter, books, and endless information.
Every day I am bombarded by the words,
opinions, and thoughts of others—things that
sound wise on the surface but largely have
absolutely nothing to do with You. The wisdom
of this world is foolishness to You. Today, when
I am tempted to listen to the world's direction,
show me Your way instead. Amen.*

Those who trust their own insight are foolish,
but anyone who walks in wisdom is safe.

PROVERBS 28:26 NLT

But the wisdom from above is first of all pure.
It is also peace loving, gentle at all times,
and willing to yield to others. It is full of
mercy and good deeds. It shows no favoritism
and is always sincere. And those who are
peacemakers will plant seeds of peace and
reap a harvest of righteousness.

JAMES 3:17–18 NLT

God, grant me the serenity to accept
the things I cannot change, the courage
to change the things I can, and the
wisdom to know the difference.

REINHOLD NIEBUHR

Light up. . .the lamp of faith in your
heart. . . . It will lead you safely
through the mists of doubt and the
black darkness of despair; along the
narrow, thorny ways of sickness and
sorrow, and over the treacherous
places of temptation and uncertainty.

JAMES ALLEN

The Fork in the Road

*What do people get for all the toil and anxious
striving with which they labor under the sun?*

ECCLESIASTES 2:22 NIV

Imagine you're approaching a fork in the
road. You're unsure of which way to turn. If
you knew ahead of time that the road to the
right would be filled with joy and the road
to the left would lead to sorrow, wouldn't it
make the decision easier? Today, as you face
multiple decisions, ask God to lead you down
the right road.

Joy in the Journey

*Father, when I read Your Word, I am
reminded that there is so much to be
learned in the journey. Why else would You
have asked Abraham and Sarah to wait so
long to have a child, or allowed the children
of Israel to wander in the wilderness for forty
years? While the promise of heaven is my final
destination, help me to find joy in the lessons
learned upon the journey. Amen.*

Wisdom is the right use of knowledge.
To know is not to be wise. Many men know
a great deal, and are all the greater fools
for it. There is no fool so great a fool as
a knowing fool. But to know how to use
knowledge is to have wisdom.

CHARLES H. SPURGEON

Maturity of mind is the capacity
to endure uncertainty.

JOHN FINLEY

The principal part of faith is patience.

GEORGE MACDONALD

JOY
in
Suffering

Therefore, since we are surrounded by such a huge crowd of witnesses to the life of faith, let us strip off every weight that slows us down. . . . Let us run with endurance. . . . We do this by keeping our eyes on Jesus, the champion who initiates and perfects our faith. Because of the joy awaiting him, he endured the cross, disregarding its shame. . . . Think of all the hostility he endured from sinful people; then you won't become weary and give up.

HEBREWS 12:1–3 NLT

Have you ever stopped to consider all the people throughout the course of history who have experienced suffering? Slavery, concentration camps, crucifixion, famine, plague, persecution. . . . If you have suffered at *any* level during your time on earth, you are in extremely good company.

The writer of Hebrews calls the believers who have suffered before us "a huge crowd of witnesses." Imagine them in heaven, seated near God, cheering us on, urging us to stay true to our faith and continue on the journey. Then, surrounded by the crowd of witnesses, when we begin to grow weary, when we feel we cannot endure one more moment of hardship, we are reminded to keep our eyes on Jesus, the ultimate Champion, who ran the race before us and proves it can be done!

Suffering is a universal human experience. Even in suffering we can experience joy, knowing that billions have gone before us and will live, eternally, to tell the tale.

The LORD says, *"I will give you back what you lost to the swarming locusts, the hopping locusts, the stripping locusts, and the cutting locusts. It was I who sent this great destroying army against you. Once again you will have all the food you want, and you will praise the LORD your God, who does these miracles for you. Never again will my people be disgraced."*

JOEL 2:25–26 NLT

My suffering was good for me, for it taught me to pay attention to your decrees.

PSALM 119:71 NLT

Learning from Suffering

*Father, I admit it. I don't like to suffer. Often it
seems my only goal in life is to avoid pain and
increase pleasure. Nonetheless, I know from
long experience that suffering is inevitable.
If it is possible for me, enable me to embrace
the pain, to gain every ounce of wisdom from
the experience as humanly and spiritually
possible, trusting You to help me endure.
Amen.*

*Dear brothers and sisters, when troubles
come your way, consider it an opportunity
for great joy. For you know that when your
faith is tested, your endurance has a chance to
grow. So let it grow, for when your endurance
is fully developed, you will be perfect
and complete, needing nothing.*

JAMES 1:2–4 NLT

*For He has not despised nor abhorred
the affliction of the afflicted; nor has He
hidden His face from him; but when he
cried to Him for help, He heard.*

PSALM 22:24 NASB

I don't think of all the misery,
but of the beauty that still remains.

ANNE FRANK

Joy is strength.

MOTHER TERESA

What a friend we have in Him.
He is always with us. When we
are depressed, He gives us joy.

CORRIE TEN BOOM

Joy is a deeply felt contentment that
transcends difficult circumstances
and derives maximum enjoyment
from every good experience.

CHARLES R. SWINDOLL

Shifting Sands

Let us hold unswervingly to the hope we profess, for he who promised is faithful.

HEBREWS 10:23 NIV

Change usually shakes us to the core. However, if you've been in a season of great suffering and you sense change is coming, you have reason to celebrate! The sands are shifting. The mourning is coming to an end. God, in His remarkable way, is reaching down with His fingertip and writing, "Look forward to tomorrow!" in the sand. Let the joy of that promise dwell in your heart. . .and bring you peace.

A Heavenly Perspective

*Lord, with my human eyes, it is difficult for me
to have a heavenly perspective on my pain.
When I am hurting, every fiber of my being just
wants it to end. However, I know that there is
a purpose for pain. If it was purposeless, You
wouldn't allow us to suffer. Help me to have a
new perspective on my suffering, help me to
view it through Your eyes. Amen.*

Then the LORD told him, "I have certainly seen the oppression of my people in Egypt. I have heard their cries of distress because of their harsh slave drivers. Yes, I am aware of their suffering. So I have come down to rescue them from the power of the Egyptians and lead them out of Egypt into their own fertile and spacious land. It is a land flowing with milk and honey—the land where the Canaanites, Hittites, Amorites, Perizzites, Hivites, and Jebusites now live."

EXODUS 3:7–8 NLT

The desires of the saints. . .are humble desires. Their hope is a humble hope; and their joy, even when it is unspeakable and full of glory, is a humble broken-hearted joy and leaves the Christian more poor in spirit and more like a little child and more disposed to a universal lowliness of behavior.

JONATHAN EDWARDS

Deep, contented joy comes from a place of complete security and confidence .(in God)—even in the midst of trial.

CHARLES R. SWINDOLL

Participate joyfully in the sorrows of the world. We cannot cure the world of sorrows, but we can choose to live in joy.

JOSEPH CAMPBELL

Come on. . .Get Happy!

*But even if you should suffer for what
is right, you are blessed. "Do not fear
their threats; do not be frightened."*
1 PETER 3:14 NIV

It's one thing to suffer because of something
you've done wrong; it's another to suffer
for doing right. Even when we're unjustly
persecuted, God wants us to respond in the
right way. If you're suffering as a result of
something you've done for the Lord. . .be
happy! Keep a stiff upper lip! This, too, shall
pass, and you *can* come through it with a
joyful attitude.

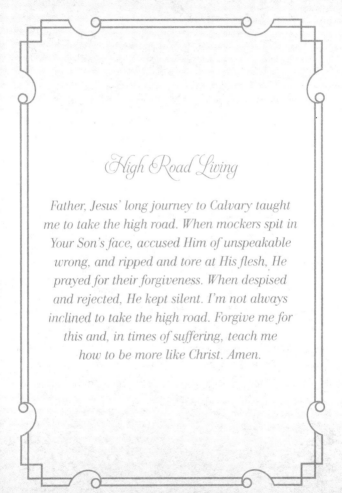

High Road Living

Father, Jesus' long journey to Calvary taught
me to take the high road. When mockers spit in
Your Son's face, accused Him of unspeakable
wrong, and ripped and tore at His flesh, He
prayed for their forgiveness. When despised
and rejected, He kept silent. I'm not always
inclined to take the high road. Forgive me for
this and, in times of suffering, teach me
how to be more like Christ. Amen.

Joy is based on the spiritual knowledge
that, while the world in which we live
is shrouded in darkness, God has
overcome the world.

HENRI J.M. NOUWEN

Joy is not necessarily the absence of
suffering, it is the presence of God.

SAM STORMS

Far better is it to dare mighty things, to win
glorious triumphs, even though checked
by failure. . .than to rank with those poor
spirits who neither enjoy much nor suffer
much, because they live in a gray twilight
that knows not victory nor defeat.

THEODORE ROOSEVELT

JOY
in
Serving

But Martha was distracted by the big dinner she was preparing. She came to Jesus and said, "Lord, doesn't it seem unfair to you that my sister [Mary] just sits here while I do all the work? Tell her to come and help me." But the Lord said to her, "My dear Martha, you are worried and upset over all these details! There is only one thing worth being concerned about."

LUKE 10:40–42 NLT

When we think of Bible passages about serving, we often think of Martha. Her keen attention to detail and foresight likely made her a fabulous party-thrower. No doubt she felt very good about her service to others. This is why it must have surprised Martha when Jesus cut through her pleas and gently pointed out that she was too focused on unimportant details.

The life of service can do this to us. Especially when we are good at serving, we can be prone to martyrdom when we don't feel that others are pulling their load. When our friends and loved ones do not share our priorities, we get sucked into black-and-white ways of thinking, entertaining thoughts such as *My way is the best way*.

Jesus certainly calls us to serve others, but He asks us to do it with a joyful, giving servant's heart, not a martyr's heart. When we become burdened by service, worried and upset about many things, it's time to check in with the Master, and get His perspective on the situation.

There are different kinds of spiritual gifts, but the same Spirit is the source of them all. There are different kinds of service, but we serve the same Lord. God works in different ways, but it is the same God who does the work in all of us.

1 Corinthians 12:4–6 nlt

You, my brothers and sisters, were called to be free. But do not use your freedom to indulge the flesh; rather, serve one another humbly in love.

Galatians 5:13 niv

If your gift is serving others, serve them well. If you are a teacher, teach well.

Romans 12:7 nlt

A Joyful Heart

*Lord, the story of Mary and Martha always
pricks my heart. I want to be like Mary, sitting
at Jesus' feet, listening to what He says. But
I'm afraid I often get caught up in the minor
details, then feel sorry for myself when others
don't do things my way. Thank You for Your
grace and for teaching me that there's a better
way. Help me to serve You from a joyful heart,
not a martyr's heart. Amen.*

God has given each of you a gift from his great variety of spiritual gifts. Use them well to serve one another.

1 Peter 4:10 NLT

"Anyone who wants to be my disciple must follow me, because my servants must be where I am. And the Father will honor anyone who serves me."

John 12:26 NLT

"For even the Son of Man came not to be served but to serve others and to give his life as a ransom for many."

Matthew 20:28 NLT

To serve is beautiful, but only if
it is done with joy and a whole
heart and a free mind.

PEARL S. BUCK

A joyful heart is the normal result
of a heart burning with love.
She gives most who gives with joy.

MOTHER TERESA

The smallest act of kindness is worth
more than the grandest intention.

OSCAR WILDE

Joy is the holy fire that keeps our purpose
warm and our intelligence aglow.

HELEN KELLER

Hem Your Blessings

Since everything God created is good, we should not reject any of it but receive it with thanks.

1 TIMOTHY 4:4 NLT.

Sometimes we walk through seasons of blessing and forget to be grateful. It's easy, with the serving of life, to overlook the fact that Someone has made provision to cover the monthly bills. Someone has graced us with good health. Someone has given us friends and loved ones to share our joys and sorrows. Today, pause a moment and thank the Lord for the many gifts He's poured out. Hem in those blessings!

Show Me Where to Serve

*Heavenly Father, it is easy to get busy doing
things I deem important under the guise of
doing them for You. It is a temptation for me
to overextend myself, to say yes to things I
shouldn't, leaving me with no margin for
anything else. The Christian life is not one of
busyness—remind me of this. Help me to find
joy in service, not in never-ending activity.*
Amen.

*Evil will slay the wicked; the foes of the
righteous will be condemned. The L*ORD
*will rescue his servants; no one who takes
refuge in him will be condemned.*

PSALM 34:21–22 NIV

*Have mercy on me, Lord, for I call to
you all day long. Bring joy to your servant,
Lord, for I put my trust in you. You, Lord,
are forgiving and good, abounding in
love to all who call to you.*

PSALM 86:3–5 NIV

*"I am the Lord's servant," Mary answered.
"May your word to me be fulfilled."*

LUKE 1:38 NIV

Man is a fallen star till he is right with heaven: he is out of order with himself and all around him till he occupies his true place in relation to God. When he serves God, he has reached that point where he doth serve himself best, and enjoys himself most. It is man's joy, it is man's heaven, to live unto God.

CHARLES H. SPURGEON

Joy is a net of love by which you can catch souls.

MOTHER TERESA

Kindness is a language which the deaf can hear and the blind can see.

MARK TWAIN

"Whoever serves me must follow me;
and where I am, my servant also will be.
My Father will honor the one who serves me."

JOHN 12:26 NIV

Who, being in very nature God, did not
consider equality with God something to be
used to his own advantage; rather, he made
himself nothing by taking the very nature
of a servant, being made in human likeness.
And being found in appearance as a man,
he humbled himself by becoming obedient
to death—even death on a cross!

PHILIPPIANS 2:6–8 NIV

JOY

in

Others

*But thank God. . . . Now he uses us to spread
the knowledge of Christ everywhere, like a sweet
perfume. Our lives are a Christ-like fragrance
rising up to God. But this fragrance is perceived
differently by those who are being saved and
by those who are perishing. To those who are
perishing, we are a dreadful smell of death and
doom. But to those who are being saved,
we are a life-giving perfume.*

2 Corinthians 2:14–16 nlt

A quick walk through the perfume section of any
upscale department store confirms the truth that
lovely scents are in the noses of the beholders.
Some people prefer light citrus scents, while others
favor musk. Some are repulsed by woodsy smells,

while others would just as soon dump a floral scent down the sink. Different noses perceive smells quite differently.

As children of God, we will always have an impact on others as we adhere to our highest calling—spreading the knowledge of Christ wherever we go. Paul likens our witness to the scent of a sweet perfume, which is so pleasing to God and His children but has the power to repulse those will ultimately reject Him.

When you are acting righteously, you may be misunderstood by others, but keep in mind their perception may have much more to do with the condition of their hearts than with you. Regardless, on this day, clothe yourself with the fragrance of Christ and find joy in others as you spread Christ's lovely, life-giving scent.

Love is patient, love is kind. It does not envy,
it does not boast, it is not proud. It does not
dishonor others, it is not self-seeking, it is not
easily angered, it keeps no record of wrongs.
Love does not delight in evil but rejoices with
the truth. It always protects, always trusts,
always hopes, always perseveres.

1 Corinthians 13:4–7 niv

Hatred stirs up quarrels,
but love makes up for all offenses.

Proverbs 10:12 nlt

To get the full value of joy, you must
have someone to divide it with.

MARK TWAIN

Scatter joy!

RALPH WALDO EMERSON

There are souls in this world who have
the gift of finding joy everywhere and
leaving it behind them when they go.

FREDERICK WILLIAM FABER

A joy shared is a joy doubled.

SWEDISH PROVERB

No Greater Joy

*I have no greater joy than to hear that
my children are walking in the truth.*

3 JOHN 4 NIV

God rejoices in a strong family. To maintain
healthiness, it's important to examine
where you all stand as individuals in your
relationship with the Lord. Sometimes we
focus on our own spiritual lives but don't pay
much attention to where our children are.
Today, ask the Lord to show you what you can
do to help your children grow in the Lord. As
they grow. . .so will your joy. And so will the
Lord's!

A Sweet Fragrance

Father, help me be a sweet fragrance to
everyone I encounter. Whether a smile on
the street or a random act of kindness, help
me to always be watchful of opportunities
to spread Your joy, Your fragrance, to others.
Thank You for entrusting me with this
responsibility and for giving me the honor
of serving You in this way. Amen.

*Whoever would foster love covers over
an offense, but whoever repeats the
matter separates close friends.*

PROVERBS 17:9 NIV

"Love your neighbor as yourself."

MATTHEW 22:39 NIV

*"But to you who are willing to listen,
I say, love your enemies! Do good to those
who hate you. Bless those who curse you.
Pray for those who hurt you."*

LUKE 6:27–28 NLT

"A new command I give you: Love one another. As I have loved you, so you must love one another. By this everyone will know that you are my disciples, if you love one another."

JOHN 13:34–35 NIV

"Greater love has no one than this:
to lay down one's life for one's friends."

JOHN 15:13 NIV

Love must be sincere. Hate what is evil; cling to what is good. Be devoted to one another in love. Honor one another above yourselves. Never be lacking in zeal, but keep your spiritual fervor, serving the Lord.

ROMANS 12:9–11 NIV

The Fruit of the Spirit

But the fruit of the Spirit is love, joy, peace,
forbearance, kindness, goodness, faithfulness.

GALATIANS 5:22 NIV

Want to know how to have the ideal family
environment? Want to see parents living
in peace with the teens, and vice versa? To
obtain a joyous family environment, you've
got to have a fruit-bowl mentality. Dealing
with anger? Reach inside the bowl for peace.
Struggling with impatience? Grab a slice
of long-suffering. Having a problem with
depression? Reach for joy. Keep that fruit bowl
close by! It's going to come in handy!

Relationships Can Be Difficult

Heavenly Father, I barely get through the beginning of the Bible before its text reminds me of a long-standing truth: Relationships can be difficult. As much as I love the people You have placed in my life, getting along with them can sometimes be an enormous challenge. Equip me to be a better family member, friend, and coworker. Enable me to be a joy to each person in my life. Amen.

*Let no debt remain outstanding, except
the continuing debt to love one another,
for whoever loves others has fulfilled the
law. The commandments, "You shall not
commit adultery," "You shall not murder,"
"You shall not steal," "You shall not covet,"
and whatever other command there may be,
are summed up in this one command:
"Love your neighbor as yourself."*

ROMANS 13:8–9 NIV

*Be completely humble and gentle;
be patient, bearing with one another in
love. Make every effort to keep the unity
of the Spirit through the bond of peace.*

EPHESIANS 4:2–3 NIV

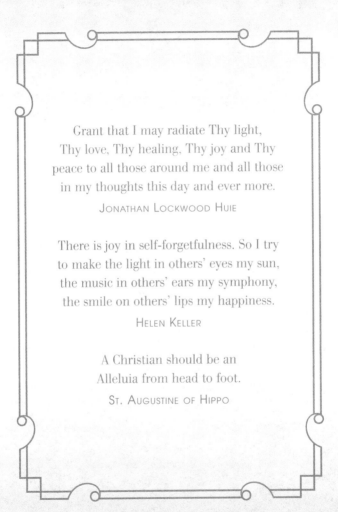

Grant that I may radiate Thy light,
Thy love, Thy healing, Thy joy and Thy
peace to all those around me and all those
in my thoughts this day and ever more.

JONATHAN LOCKWOOD HUIE

There is joy in self-forgetfulness. So I try
to make the light in others' eyes my sun,
the music in others' ears my symphony,
the smile on others' lips my happiness.

HELEN KELLER

A Christian should be an
Alleluia from head to foot.

ST. AUGUSTINE OF HIPPO

This is a great mystery, but it is an illustration of the way Christ and the church are one. So again I say, each man must love his wife as he loves himself, and the wife must respect her husband.

EPHESIANS 5:32–33 NLT

If you have any encouragement from being united with Christ, if any comfort from his love, if any common sharing in the Spirit, if any tenderness and compassion, then make my joy complete by being like-minded, having the same love, being one in spirit and of one mind. Do nothing out of selfish ambition or vain conceit.

PHILIPPIANS 2:1–3 NIV

JOY
in
Abundance

"The next seven years will be a period of great prosperity throughout the land of Egypt."

GENESIS 41:29 NLT

We understand the need to cry out to God when we are facing disaster, loss, or lack of physical provision. In fact, it is often quite natural to turn to the Lord in times of suffering. It can be more of a challenge to turn to Him in times of abundance, to ask for wisdom as to how to use our blessings to serve Him.

Joseph was as acquainted with plenty as he was poverty. Whether he was persecuted and rejected by his brothers at the bottom of a well or forgotten in prison, Joseph learned to seek God's face in times of adversity. Wisdom enabled him to turn to God in better times as well. When Pharaoh was confused by perplexing dreams, he had Joseph released from prison and brought to him. Joseph, leaning on the wisdom of God, interpreted Pharaoh's dream and instructed the Egyptian king to act conservatively. He advised Pharaoh to store crops in the good years so there would be enough food for the people in the lean years. "Otherwise this famine will destroy the land" (Genesis 41:36 NLT). And, of course, Joseph's predictions came to fruition, saving not only the Egyptians but his father and brothers.

God certainly wants us to cherish times of blessing, but true joy is found in using our abundance wisely, to honor Him and help others.

"From the dew of heaven and the richness of the earth, may God always give you abundant harvests of grain and bountiful new wine."

GENESIS 27:28 NLT

"The LORD will send rain at the proper time from his rich treasury in the heavens and will bless all the work you do. You will lend to many nations, but you will never need to borrow from them."

DEUTERONOMY 28:12 NLT

You make known to me the path of life; you will fill me with joy in your presence, with eternal pleasures at your right hand.

PSALM 16:11 NIV

To rejoice in temporal comforts is
dangerous, to rejoice in self is foolish,
to rejoice in sin is fatal, but to
rejoice in God is heavenly.

CHARLES H. SPURGEON

The sun does not shine for a few trees
and flowers but for the wide world's joy.

HENRY WARD BEECHER

People from a planet without flowers
would think we must be mad with joy the
whole time to have such things about us.

IRIS MURDOCH

Daily Provision

*"Who provides food for the raven
when its young cry out to God and
wander about for lack of food?"*

JOB 38:41 NIV

Does it fill your heart with joy to know that
God provides for your needs? He makes
provision. . .both in seasons of want and
seasons of plenty. There's no need to strive.
No need to worry. He's got it all under control.
If He provides food for the ravens, then surely
He knows how to give you everything you
need when you need it. So, praise Him!

Thank You for Blessing

Heavenly Father, thank You for Your blessings!
Thank You for knowing me intimately,
down to the number of hairs on my head.
I thank You for meeting my spiritual, physical,
and emotional needs. Help me to remember
You in times of blessing. I know that every
good and perfect gift comes from You.
In return, I bring to You myself and all
I have as an offering of praise. Amen.

Rejoice in the Lord always.
I will say it again: Rejoice!

PHILIPPIANS 4:4 NIV

"The LORD your God is with you, the Mighty
Warrior who saves. He will take great delight
in you; in his love he will no longer rebuke
you, but will rejoice over you with singing."

ZEPHANIAH 3:17 NIV

Taste and see that the LORD is good;
blessed is the one who takes refuge in him.

PSALM 34:8 NIV

Carpe diem! Rejoice while you are alive,
enjoy the day; live life to the fullest,
make the most of what you have.

HORACE

To be rich in admiration and free from
envy, to rejoice greatly in the good
of others, to love with such generosity
of heart that your love is still a dear
possession in absence or unkindness, these
are the gifts which money can't buy.

ROBERT LOUIS STEVENSON

Extraordinary Blessing

"There will be showers of blessing."
EZEKIEL 34:26 NIV

Don't you enjoy walking through seasons of extraordinary blessing? We can hardly believe it when God's "more than enough" (Exodus 36:7 NASB) provision shines down upon us. What did we do to deserve it? Nothing! During such seasons, we can't forget to thank Him for the many ways He is moving in our lives. Our hearts must overflow with gratitude to a gracious and almighty God.

Scatter Joy

Maker of heaven and earth, You are creative
beyond my imagination, wild with abundance.
Thank You for the spring rains, for the flower's
bloom, for the sweet reminders of Your
presence that surround me every day. Help
me to rejoice in Your abundance, to treasure
Your attention to detail and to spread that joy
extravagantly, just as You do. Amen.

Then Christ will make his home in your hearts as you trust in him. Your roots will grow down into God's love and keep you strong. And may you have the power to understand, as all God's people should, how wide, how long, how high, and how deep his love is. May you experience the love of Christ, though it is too great to understand fully. Then you will be made complete with all the fullness of life and power that comes from God.

EPHESIANS 3:17–19 NLT

JOY
in
Simplicity

"Very truly I tell you, the Son can do nothing by himself; he can do only what he sees his Father doing, because whatever the Father does the Son also does."
JOHN 5:19 NIV

In 1896, evangelist and preacher Charles Sheldon wrote a powerful novel called *In His Steps*. Its premise was simple. Before embarking on any task, before making any decision, the pastor in the story compelled members of his congregation to ask themselves one simple question: What would Jesus do? A century later, long before viral videos and flash mobs, this simple concept grew like wildfire. Soon, bracelets, T-shirts, and bumper stickers bore the simple letters *WWJD*.

How would it simplify our lives to ask ourselves this question? If Jesus approached us and asked us to "drop our nets"—leave our families, possessions, and livelihoods—and follow Him, would we do so? Of course, Jesus didn't have children, a home with a mortgage, or summer vacation plans to make—He could come and go a little more freely than we, who have a myriad of belongings and obligations, are wont to do. His was definitely a life of simplicity, one that afforded Him the freedom to do his Father's will, to come and go as the moment and His children required. Jesus arranged His life around His Father's wishes and desires. If you long for the joy of a simpler life, ask yourself one simple question: What would Jesus do?

*Your laws are wonderful. No wonder I obey
them! The teaching of your word gives light,
so even the simple can understand. I pant with
expectation, longing for your commands.*

PSALM 119:129–131 NLT

*I have learned to be content whatever the
circumstances. I know what it is to be in need,
and I know what it is to have plenty. I have
learned the secret of being content in any and
every situation, whether well fed or hungry,
whether living in plenty or in want.*

PHILIPPIANS 4:11–12 NIV

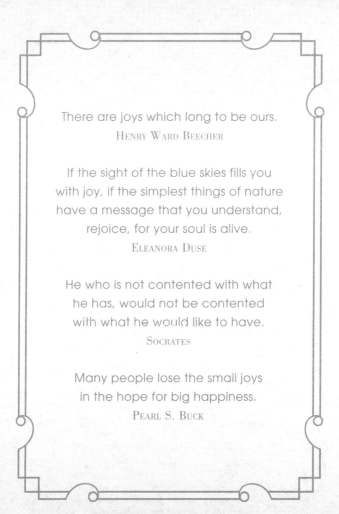

There are joys which long to be ours.

HENRY WARD BEECHER

If the sight of the blue skies fills you
with joy, if the simplest things of nature
have a message that you understand,
rejoice, for your soul is alive.

ELEANORA DUSE

He who is not contented with what
he has, would not be contented
with what he would like to have.

SOCRATES

Many people lose the small joys
in the hope for big happiness.

PEARL S. BUCK

Who Provides?

*"Consider the lilies, how they grow:
they neither toil nor spin."*

LUKE 12:27 NASB

Sometimes we look at our job as our provision.
We say things like, "I work for my money."
While it's true that we work hard (and are
rewarded with a paycheck) we can't forget that
God is our provider. If He cares for the lilies of
the field, flowers that bloom for such a short
season, then how much more does He care
for us, His children? What joy. . .realizing God
loves us enough to provide for our needs.

Contentment in Simplicity

Father, I am bombarded with the message that I need more! More clothes, more friends, more fun, more of everything. Yet I know that I do not need more, for in You I truly have everything! Cultivate within me a spirit of contentment. Help me to be satisfied—better yet, joyful—with the blessings You have already given me, knowing You give me more than I could ever desire. Amen.

After all, we brought nothing with us when we came into the world, and we can't take anything with us when we leave it. So if we have enough food and clothing, let us be content. But people who long to be rich fall into temptation and are trapped by many foolish and harmful desires that plunge them into ruin and destruction.

1 TIMOTHY 6:7–9 NLT

Keep your lives free from the love of money and be content with what you have.

HEBREWS 13:5 NIV

I sometimes wonder whether all
pleasures are not substitutes for joy.
C. S. LEWIS

Laughter is a sunbeam of the soul.
THOMAS MANN

Wondrous as it is, how simple is this
mystery! To love Christ and to
know that I love Him—this is all!
ELIZABETH PRENTISS

A flower blossoms for its own joy.
OSCAR WILDE

Joyful in Love

Keep yourselves in the love of God,
waiting anxiously for the mercy of
our Lord Jesus Christ to eternal life.

JUDE 21 NASB

When you love the Lord and recognize His
great love for you, it's easy to be joyful!
Think of His marvelous deeds. Relish in His
overwhelming love for His children. Recognize
His daily blessings. Oh, may we never forget
that the Lord our God longs for us to see the
depth of His love for us. . .and to love Him
fully in return.

Perspective

Heavenly Father, please forgive me for looking to people, possessions, and activities to fill the empty places in my soul. I invest so much energy in trying to get my needs met in temporal ways. When I feel restless, empty, and bored, remind me that You are the only one who could ever truly satisfy me. Thank You for meeting my needs— and wants—as only You can do. Amen.

*Yet true godliness with contentment
is itself great wealth.*

1 TIMOTHY 6:6 NLT

*The LORD is my shepherd, I lack nothing.
He makes me lie down in green pastures,
he leads me beside quiet waters, he refreshes
my soul. He guides me along the right
paths for his name's sake.*

PSALM 23:1–3 NIV

*The fruit of that righteousness will
be peace; its effect will be quietness
and confidence forever.*

ISAIAH 32:17 NIV

JOY
in
Worship

Come, let us bow down in worship,
let us kneel before the LORD our Maker;
for he is our God and we are the people
of his pasture, the flock under his care.

PSALM 95:6–7 NIV

On the day Jacob said a final good-bye to his son Joseph, Jacob worshipped. On the day the Israelites learned that God had remembered them in their misery and was deeply concerned for their well-being, they fell to their knees and worshipped. On the day Hannah brought her son Samuel to the Lord's service, she worshipped, no doubt through tears. On the day Shadrach, Meshach, and Abednego were threatened with their lives, they refused to worship *anyone* but the Lord their God.

Scripture tells the stories of thousands of days of striving and pain and joy and loss, and through it all, from the dawn of creation to the dream of heaven, one bright thread connects them all—worship.

We are God's people. He has numbered each and every one of our days—knowing full well they would be filled with joy and sorrow and laughter and pain. He accounts for each of those days and each of our tears. There is never one day, one moment, when we are not under His care.

When we are without words, without strength, or filled to the brim with all the good things He has given, our only response is to fall to our knees and worship our God, Creator, Majesty, King of all kings, Lord of all lords. There is no greater joy.

"You must worship no other gods, for the LORD, whose very name is Jealous, is a God who is jealous about his relationship with you."

"You alone are the LORD. You made the heavens, even the highest heavens, and all their starry host, the earth and all that is on it, the seas and all that is in them. You give life to everything, and the multitudes of heaven worship you."

When we lift our hands in praise and
worship, we break spiritual jars of
perfume over Jesus. The fragrance
of our praise fills the whole earth
and touches the heart of God.
DENNIS IGNATIUS

Joyful, joyful we adore thee, God of Glory
Lord of Love; hearts unfold like flowers
before Thee, opening to the sun above.
Melt the clouds of sun and sadness, drive
the dark of doubt away. Giver of immortal
gladness, fill us with the light of day.
HENRY VAN DYKE

Thou dost ever lead Thine own
in the love of joys unknown.
MARTIN JANUS

Joy. . .a Powerful Force

Praise the LORD! Praise God in His sanctuary;
praise Him in His mighty expanse.

PSALM 150:1 KJV

There's just something amazing about being
in a powerful worship service when all of
God's children are like-minded, lifting up
their voices in joyful chorus. The next time
you're in such a service, pause a moment and
listen. . .really listen. Can you sense the joy
that sweeps across the room? The wonder?
Oh, what a powerful force we are when we
praise in one accord!

My Bursting Heart

Father, what a joy it is to be called Your child.
My heart bursts with love for You as I raise
my hands in joyful praise. I pray that my life,
each day, would be a reflection of Your love
for me, that I would spread Your joy to others,
lavishly. I look forward to an eternity of
praising You. Amen.

Ascribe to the LORD, O sons of the mighty,
ascribe to the LORD glory and strength.
Ascribe to the LORD the glory due to
His name; worship the LORD in holy array.

PSALM 29:1–3 NASB

Therefore God exalted him to the highest
place and gave him the name that is above
every name, that at the name of Jesus every
knee should bow, in heaven and on earth ·
and under the earth, and every tongue
acknowledge that Jesus Christ is Lord,
to the glory of God the Father.

PHILIPPIANS 2:9–11 NIV

The greatest joy of a Christian
is to give joy to Christ.

CHARLES H. SPURGEON

Joy can be real only if people look
upon their life as a service, and have a
definite object in life outside themselves
and their personal happiness.

LEO TOLSTOY

Joy to the world, the Lord is come. . . .
Let heaven and nature sing.

ISAAC WATTS

Go Out with Joy

*"For you will go out with joy and be led forth
with peace; the mountains and the hills will
break forth into shouts of joy before you, and
all the trees of the field will clap their hands."*

ISAIAH 55:12 NASB

God reveals Himself in a million different
ways, but perhaps the most breathtaking is
through nature. The next time you're in a
mountainous spot, pause and listen. Can you
hear the sound of God's eternal song? Does joy
radiate through your being? Aren't you filled
with wonder and with peace? The Lord has,
through the beauty of nature, given us a rare
and glorious gift.

The Beauty All Around Me

Heavenly Father, when I see the stars across the night sky, feel the power of crashing ocean waves, or breathe in cool mountain air, I am astounded by Your beauty. I am amazed that You, the Creator of the universe, cares enough to call me His own. What a joy it is to be Your child, to experience Your love through the beauty of Your creation. Thank You for this unspeakable joy. Amen.

Lord, our Lord, how majestic is your name
in all the earth! You have set your glory in
the heavens. Through the praise of children
and infants you have established a stronghold
against your enemies, to silence the foe and
the avenger. When I consider your heavens,
the work of your fingers, the moon and the
stars, which you have set in place, what is
mankind that you are mindful of them,
human beings that you care for them?

Psalm 8:1–4 NIV

JOY

in

the

Storm

When it snows, she has no fear
for her household; for all of
them are clothed in scarlet.

PROVERBS 31:21 NIV

Imagine a storm is coming. It's the blizzard of the century. Jane overhears someone talking about it but, between her work, children, and other obligations, the news barely registers. When she wakes up the next morning to three feet of snow and no hope of getting out the driveway, her heart fills with dread. There's no milk. There's no bread. And although she'd meant to call a furnace repairperson all week, she hadn't had the time.

The day before, her neighbor, Joy, had also heard about the storm. So while she had the children bring in wood for the fire, she made a quick trip to the grocery store. She cancelled the family's plans for the next day and brought a stack of games and books up from the basement. She went to bed that night, eagerly anticipating the fun of a snow day.

Depending on how well we are prepared, storms can be a tragedy or a minor interruption to a busy life. Expecting storms to come our way doesn't change them, but it *can* lessen their impact. In John 16:33, Jesus told His disciples, "In this world you will have trouble" (NIV). Storms *will* come. And just as physical preparation helps us manage earthly storms, spiritual preparation helps us weather the inevitable emotional storms that Jesus said would come our way. But take heart. Whether you are prepared or not, Jesus will help you ride out each and every kind of tempest. Looking to Him, you can have joy in any storm.

*O Lord God of Heaven's Armies! Where is
there anyone as mighty as you, O Lord?
You are entirely faithful. You rule the oceans.
You subdue their storm-tossed waves. You
crushed the great sea monster. You scattered
your enemies with your mighty arm.*

Psalm 89:8–10 nlt

*When the storms of life come,
the wicked are whirled away,
but the godly have a lasting foundation.*

Proverbs 10:25 nlt

162

Those who have the wind of the Holy Spirit
in their souls glide ahead even while they
sleep. If the vessel of our soul is still being
tossed by wind or storms, we should wake
the Lord who has been resting with us all
along, and He will swiftly calm the sea.

BROTHER LAWRENCE

Storms in their fury may rage all around,
I have peace, sweet peace.

HALDOR LILLENAS

For after all, the best thing one
can do when it is raining is let it rain.

HENRY WADSWORTH LONGFELLOW

A Joyous Defense

But let all who take refuge in you be glad;
let them ever sing for joy. Spread your
protection over them, that those who love
your name may rejoice in you.

PSALM 5:11 NIV

Oh, the pain of betrayal. If you've been hurt
by someone you trusted, choose to release
that person today. Let it go. God is your
defender. He's got your back. Take refuge in
Him. And remember, praising Him even in
the storm will shift your focus back where it
belongs. Praise the Lord! He is our defense!

A Promise amid the Storm

Lord, it is difficult for me to prepare for life's storms. I'd rather have clear, sunny weather every single day. But Your Word warns me that there will be trouble. Prepare my heart to effectively endure life's storms. Help me not to live in denial but instead to cling to the promise that You have overcome the world.
Amen.

But you are a tower of refuge to the poor, O
LORD, a tower of refuge to the needy in distress.
You are a refuge from the storm and
a shelter from the heat.

ISAIAH 25:4 NLT

Then the LORD will provide shade for Mount
Zion and all who assemble there. He will
provide a canopy of cloud during the day and
smoke and flaming fire at night, covering the
glorious land. It will be a shelter from daytime
heat and a hiding place from storms and rain.

ISAIAH 4:5–6 NLT

Life isn't finding shelter in the storm.
It's about learning to dance in the rain.
SHERRILYN KENYON

There are some things you learn
best in calm, and some in storm.
WILLA CATHER

Don't worry about a thing, 'cause
every little thing gonna be all right.
BOB MARLEY

I am not afraid of storms,
for I am learning how to sail my ship.
LOUISA MAY ALCOTT

Rooted and Grounded

*"Those on the rocky ground are the ones who
receive the word with joy when they hear it,
but they have no root. They believe for a while,
but in the time of testing they fall away."*

LUKE 8:13 NIV

Imagine a sturdy oak tree, one that's been
growing for decades. Its roots run deep. It's
grounded. When the storms of life strike,
that tree is going to stand strong. Now think
of your own roots. Do they run deep? When
temptations strike, will you stand strong? Dig
into the Word. Receive it with joy. Let it be
your foundation. Plant yourself and let your
roots run deep.

Awareness of Your Presence

Jesus, when I read about the disciples' fear
in the storm on the lake, I wonder how they
could be so afraid with You right there in
the boat. Didn't they know You are the Lord
of the earth and sea? Yet sometimes I, too,
become afraid, forgetting that You are with
me always, that You never leave my side.
Through foul and fair weather, Lord, increase
my awareness of Your presence. Amen.

"Lord, help!" they cried in their trouble,
and he saved them from their distress.
He calmed the storm to a whisper and stilled
the waves. What a blessing was that stillness
as he brought them safely into harbor!

PSALM 107:28–30 NLT

Suddenly, a fierce storm struck the lake,
with waves breaking into the boat. But Jesus
was sleeping. The disciples went and woke
him up, shouting, "Lord, save us! We're going
to drown!" Jesus responded, "Why are you
afraid? You have so little faith!" Then he got
up and rebuked the wind and waves,
and suddenly there was a great calm.

MATTHEW 8:24–26 NLT

JOY
in
Waiting

The LORD said to Moses, "Come up to me on the mountain and stay here, and I will give you the tablets of stone with the law and commandments I have written for their instruction." Then Moses set out with Joshua his aide, and Moses went up on the mountain of God. He said to the elders, "Wait here for us until we come back to you."

EXODUS 24:12–14 NIV

Waiting can feel eternal, especially when we don't know exactly how long the wait will be. For the children of Israel, who ended up waiting their whole lives, the forty days and forty nights Moses spent on the mountain must have seemed like a very long time, made even worse because Moses didn't say exactly just how long he would be gone.

So they found some things to do to pass the time, like making and worshipping a golden calf. Aaron managed to spin the event as "a festival to the Lord" (Exodus 32:5 NIV). But Scripture tells us it was revelry, and God said His people had become corrupt.

It probably doesn't matter whether it was boredom, lack of faith, or willful disobedience that allowed the Israelites to disregard God so blatantly. The bottom line is that God was extremely angry and disappointed by their actions, and they missed an important chance to demonstrate their faith in Him.

Are you waiting for something today? If so, be sure not to allow boredom, lack of faith, or willful disobedience rob you of a valuable opportunity to seek God's face and demonstrate Your patient devotion—to Him and Him alone.

*Hear my cry for help, my King and my God,
for to you I pray. In the morning, L*ORD*, you
hear my voice; in the morning I lay my
requests before you and wait expectantly.*

PSALM 5:2–3 NIV

*Yet I am confident I will see the L*ORD*'s
goodness while I am here in the land of the
living. Wait patiently for the L*ORD*. Be brave and
courageous. Yes, wait patiently for the L*ORD*.*

PSALM 27:13–14 NLT

Restlessness and impatience change
nothing except our peace and joy.
Peace does not dwell in outward things,
but in the heart prepared to wait trustfully
and quietly on Him who has all things
safely in His hands.

ELISABETH ELLIOT

When we are powerless to do a thing,
it is a great joy that we can come
and step inside the ability of Jesus.

CORRIE TEN BOOM

The greater part of our happiness
or misery depends on our dispositions
and not upon our circumstances.

MARTHA WASHINGTON

The Fruit of Your Labor

You will eat the fruit of your labor;
blessings and prosperity will be yours.
PSALM 128:2 NIV

We're always waiting for the payoff, aren't we?
When we've put a lot of effort into a project,
for example, we hope to see good results.
The Word of God promises that we will eat
the fruit of our labor, that we will eventually
experience blessings and prosperity. So
all of that hard work will be worth it. But
remember, the joy is in the journey! It's not
just in the payoff.

Teach Me to Wait

Father, waiting is hard. I become restless,
impatient. I wonder if you have forgotten me.
My mind starts to wander and I forget Your
promises. Then I begin to doubt whether I
have really heard You at all. Teach me to wait,
Lord. Teach me to wait for You and on You.
Help me to use waiting as an opportunity
to learn from You. Amen.

I say to myself, "The Lord is my inheritance; therefore, I will hope in him!" The Lord is good to those who depend on him, to those who search for him. So it is good to wait quietly for salvation from the Lord.

Lamentations 3:24–26 NLT

"But those who hope in the Lord will renew their strength. They will soar on wings like eagles; they will run and not grow weary, they will walk and not be faint."

Isaiah 40:31 NIV

If you have overcome your inclination,
and not been overcome by it,
you have reason to rejoice.

PLAUTUS

Does everything in my life fill his heart with
gladness, or do I constantly complain
because things don't seem to be going
my way? A person who has forgotten what
God treasures will not be filled with joy.

OSWALD CHAMBERS

Time is very slow for those who wait,
very fast for those who are scared,
very long for those who lament,
very short for those who celebrate,
but for those who love, time is eternal.

WILLIAM SHAKESPEARE

Disappointment. . .Be Gone!

*And this hope will not
lead to disappointment.*
ROMANS 5:5 NLT

Tired of being disappointed time and time
again? Ready for things to change? Try hope.
Hope never leads to disappointment. When
you're hopeful, you are anticipating good
things, not bad. And even if the "good things"
you're waiting on don't happen right away,
you're energized with joy until they do. So,
wave good-bye to disappointment. Choose
hope. Choose joy.

Waiting for the Right Things

*Father, I spend so much time waiting for
temporal things. I wait for checks to arrive,
for my turn at the window, for a loved one to
say, "I'm sorry. . . ." Your word reminds me to
wait for eternal things—You, Your gift, Your
Son, Your Spirit, the blessed hope to which You
have called me. Lord, as I wait for You below,
set my heart and sight on things above. Amen.*

So God has given both his promise and his oath. These two things are unchangeable because it is impossible for God to lie. Therefore, we who have fled to him for refuge can have great confidence as we hold to the hope that lies before us. This hope is a strong and trustworthy anchor for our souls. It leads us through the curtain into God's inner sanctuary. Jesus has already gone in there for us. He has become our eternal High Priest in the order of Melchizedek.

HEBREWS 6:18–20 NLT

JOY in the
Hope

of

Heaven

*"Don't store up treasures here on earth,
where moths eat them and rust destroys
them, and where thieves break in and steal.
Store your treasures in heaven, where moths
and rust cannot destroy, and thieves do not
break in and steal. Wherever your treasure is,
there the desires of your heart will also be."*
MATTHEW 6:19–21 NLT

When the days are long, it is hard to remember
that this world is temporary. It is not our home.
Although we tend to put enormous effort into living
our best life here on earth, Jesus reminds us that it
is foolish to store our treasures here. Every earthly
thing we work so hard for will eventually be gone.

I thank my God for graciously granting
me the opportunity of learning that
death is the key which unlocks the
door to our true happiness.

WOLFGANG AMADEUS MOZART

We may speak about a place where there
are no tears, no death, no fear, no night;
but those are just the benefits of heaven.
The beauty of heaven is seeing God.

MAX LUCADO

I have come home at last! This is my
real country! I belong here. This is the
land I have been looking for all my life,
though I never knew it till now. . . .
Come further up, come further in!

C. S. LEWIS

The Joy of Heaven

*"I saw the Lord sitting on His throne,
and all the host of heaven standing
on His right and on His left."*

2 Chronicles 18:18 NASB

What do you think of when you ponder the
word *heaven*? What will it be like to walk on
streets of gold, to see our loved ones who have
gone before us? How thrilling to know we will
one day meet our Lord and Savior face-to-face.
He has gone to prepare a place for us, and
what a place it will be! The joy of eternity is
ours as believers. Praise Him!

Joy for Today, Joy for Eternity

*Father, I'm not the best at delayed
gratification. I often want the good things now,
no waiting. Your word reminds me that I can
have the good things now, and for eternity!
The secret is abiding in You and choosing joy,
regardless of what this days brings. Thank You
for this moment in time, preparing me for the
day I will spend eternity with You. Amen.*

For the Lord Himself will descend from
heaven with a shout, with the voice of the
archangel and with the trumpet of God,
and the dead in Christ will rise first.
Then we who are alive and remain will
be caught up together with them in the
clouds to meet the Lord in the air,
and so we shall always be with the Lord.

1 Thessalonians 4:16–17 NASB